FM 99-100

Sergeant Shenk's Comprehensive Book on Knife Throwing

By Timothy J. Shenk
US Army (retired)

Copyright © 2010 by Timothy J. Shenk Sr.
All cheesy artwork by Timothy J. Shenk Sr.
All rights reserved.

No part of this book may be reproduced in any form or by any electronic or mechanical means including information storage and retrieval systems, without permission in writing from the author: exception for short quotes for a review. Thanks.

Special thanks to Amy; my friend and editor.

Contact at: SFCshenk@gmail.com

The **FM** in the book title does not stand for the US Army's "Field Manual" designation – but stands for "Fun" Manual.

CONTENTS

FOREWORD

CHAPTER 1 - SAFETY FIRST

CHAPTER 2 – KNIVES AND THROWING IMPLEMENTS

CHAPTER 3 – COLLECTING AND MODIFYING THROWING KNIVES

CHAPTER 4 - TARGETS

CHAPTER 5 – THROWING TECHNIQUES

a long time ago

Foreword

What This Book Can and
What This Book Can Not Do For You

My goal is to impart all I know from 35 years of avid knife throwing. How good am I at throwing knives? I miss... occasionally. While I don't lose sleep over it; I don't like to miss so I try to determine the reason why I missed. Like a knife's edge – precision knife throwing requires constant honing as the cares of daily life can wear one's edge and focus dull.

While this book can not make you a pro knife thrower in a day - or probably not even a week (it took me years and a lot of busted knives) - it can help by saving you significant time in the learning process and money in busted knives and maybe legal charges or stitches. In this regard, you'll learn much faster and easier than I did. If there is a trick to precision knife throwing, that would be knowing how the knife must spin in flight and visualizing that spin: More on this in chapter 5. That aside, there's no substitute for frequent practice – as often as possible and always safely.

I have read other books on knife throwing and, if nothing else, greatly enjoyed reading the thoughts and advice of other men like myself, who for some primordial reason are totally hooked on whipping knives into things. In my opinion, their techniques are as good as mine (and not much different) - it comes down to your developing your own individual style. Still, there is bound to be something to be learned from any thrower with thirty-five years of observation, trial and error, and practice at knife throwing. This is what I shall impart in this book.

Sergeant Shenk's Knife Throwing Story

Combat soldier - knife thrower? As a combat leader I usually had a radio to call a fire support mission, a rifle, machinegun or an M1 tank as my primary weapons, and a pistol, grenades, boots, dukes, knives and jelly bean offerings for backup weapons. Today, knives carried by combat soldiers are more often for use as tools and toys than weapons – and they were in my army days as well… for the *most* part. But unlike the vast array of modern weapons, a knife never jams, misfires, or mistakes its target.

Not counting my army-issue bayonet, I carried three personal knives in the field: one dainty but very sharp gentleman's knife for opening my MRE's and dressing foot blisters from the march, one Leatherman multi-tool for taking apart and fixing weapons and gear, and a venerable Camillus Air Force issue (though I was army) Pilot's Survival knife - for throwing.

The Camillus Pilot's issue knife was for years my personal favorite for throwing - and it was made very durable. Though not a full-tang knife, the Camillus USAF Pilot's issue knife is unique in that it is tempered very hard in the point but made softer and actually quite pliable towards the handle end; so the knife's point had great penetration capabilities but the knife handle would bend before it broke and could be easily bent back. When I was an infantry grunt, I also was required to carry the issue bayonet at the time – the M9 Phrobis - damn things are as heavy as two railroad spikes and subsequently hit hard like a thrown javelin – but highly prone to boomerang back at high velocities. As a rule, I didn't throw my issue stuff; if you broke or lost it you'd have to answer for it and maybe pay for it - what Uncle Sam paid for it.

In my first four-year hitch, I was a paratrooper in the 82nd Airborne Division at Fort Bragg. The senior leadership (those usually in the rear with the beer) officially frowned on knife throwing because invariably some unlearned, careless young soldier would make a bad throw and somebody (maybe himself) would get punctured. It was made clear - knife throwing was strictly not allowed. So when we were out in the field, only after I made sure the leadership wasn't around, I threw knives - all the time - and we were in the field most of the year - day in and day out – fair or foul weather. So I broke regulations and threw knives and taught a few others to throw knives - or at least got them interested. Word got around that I was a knife thrower.

One day, my platoon had just returned to the barracks from a lengthy stay in the field. Our gear and weapons were accounted for, cleaned, inspected, and turned in and we were waiting to be dismissed for the weekend (life's simple pleasures and conveniences were never so good as after a long, hot, bug-eaten, dirty stay in the field). I was lounging around outside the barracks when my platoon sergeant - a man we knew as Wild Bill, as he was quite a wild card - approached me.

Wild Bill was older than most of us, very humorous, but "harder (as he used to say) than woodpecker lips" as a soldier - meaning he was tough, quick, intelligent, and cut no slack. So we liked and respected the man as a great tactical leader but yet a real joker - his wit and observation skills were razor sharp. As he approached me, I saw that he had a look of business about him. Because I was a private then, I snapped to parade rest as he addressed me.

"So Shenk, I hear you are quite a knife thrower." He said with a dry grin.

Now I am in a spot. I knew it was made clear - no knife throwing. I thought about it - It was true I was a knife thrower – but I wasn't "quite a knife thrower". I missed often enough.

"That's not true Sergeant."

He continued to grin and said, "Come on, I heard you are really good throwing a knife."

I continued to tell him I wasn't and that I couldn't understand who would tell him such a thing - some kind of far-fetched story.

To this, he said, "I've got a platoon leader meeting to make. I want you out here in a half an hour with your knives and then you show me what you can do." It wasn't a request but an order. And he walked off into the barracks.

I was in a dilemma. Knife throwing was against rules and this was a strict unit. Some slight infractions could result in relatively heavy consequences. Well, I figured I had no choice - I'd get my trusty Camillus knife and meet him - throw the damn thing a couple times and most likely miss and that would be that. I'd be more careful in the future who saw me throwing knives out in the field.

It was a hot summer North Carolina day when I met Sergeant Wild Bill behind out barracks. I had my venerable Camillus knife. The sun was oppressively bright as I recall. Bill picked up an empty cigarette pack off the ground, walked over to a huge plywood bulletin board and tacked the pack there upon it and came back to where I was standing - about 25 feet away from the target. He stood next to me and looked pretty happy - as if he felt he was in for a show. There was just no way I was going to even hit the cigarette pack with my knife - let alone hit it point first. This was going to be pathetic.

"OK, show me your stuff Shenk." Wild Bill said, as he stood there cross armed and staring at the cigarette pack target – awaiting and expecting an exhibition of greatness.

Rather feebly - with zero confidence, I threw the knife in the general direction and you know I nailed that pack - hard – point first - dead center! The Camillus sunk in solid - right through the center of pack and splintered halfway out the other side of the board it was tacked to!

I was really just stunned, amazed at my lucky-ass throw! But I played it off with false calm and confidence as if that was my normal skill level. I said nothing as I stood there trying to look as if my secret had been revealed: Wild Bill also didn't look surprised as he was apparently expecting nothing less. I was hoping Wild Bill wouldn't ask me to do this again. He didn't. Instead he was looking angry.

"Don't you ever lie to me again about your skills Shenk; you understand me?" He was sincerely upset. "You can bullshit the other guys all you like – but not me. Is that clear?"

"Yes Sergeant!" was the reply military protocol required and that is what I said. But he wasn't through.

"Shenk, you are now first platoon's designated Silent Sentry Take-Out Man; and don't you ever lie to me again." Then he walked off.

Silent Sentry Take-Out Man?! What? Why who ever heard of such a thing? It would be funny if I was anything but a paratrooper in Wild Bill's platoon – why, he'd have me do it! If we went to combat, and my unit had a lengthy and active combat history, and there was an enemy needing taken out with stealth – *knife style*, well, Wild Bill was certainly the sort to order me out to do it. OK, but thing was, I wasn't that damn good! Hitting that pack square on like I did must have been about the dumb luckiest throw I'd ever made in my life at that point; or it was guided by Divine help.

So as I retrieved my knife, I stood there thinking about my brand new fancy job description - *Silent Sentry Take-Out Man*, and I couldn't bring myself to laugh at the whole thing though a large part of me wanted to. Instead I had a slight sinking feeling in my stomach: he would have me do this in a combat situation – I knew he would.

I knew what I had to do: I had to really apply myself at mastering knife throwing as my division, the 82nd Airborne, had a mission to be anywhere on the globe within 17 hours of being called up. I got serious about learning to throw knives with dependable accuracy and I've been at it ever since.

Thankfully, I never had to take out any sentries - *at least not yet!*

Why Throw a Knife?

1. Knife throwing is *sexy*!
That's right, knife throwing IS sexy.
I have never met a woman yet that didn't think my unusual skill at throwing a knife was something uncommonly cool about me – just another reason to date me – to date the knife-throwing man.

Don't take my word for it. It's on TV so it's got to be true. Hollywood has a long-standing love-affair with knife throwers; and most of them are portrayed as something special. Notice that they are all very lean and gritty-looking; Bill the Butcher of *Gangs of New York* and Mick of *Crocodile Dundee* come to my mind; there are many more. They all seem to share some strong, dark, brooding personality. Maybe you do too. What's the appeal of knife throwing?

Obviously every person who takes up mastering knife throwing has his or her distinct reasons. For me, aside from being a sexy hobby and the designated First Platoon Silent Sentry Take-Out Man, it was and still is the challenge of taking the bullshit luck factor out of throwing and hitting the target: point-first consistently at many given ranges.

2. Knife Throwing is a Precision Martial Art.

Invariably house burglaries come and go in my area. Now and then they turned violent with tragic consequences. I considered getting a pistol but thought about it: with kids and adult friends who act like kids, I am not too keen on loaded handguns in my place. I knew within the ranges found in my house (15 feet or less), I could accurately throw a knife as quick (probably quicker) as I could grab, charge, aim and shoot a pistol; and with equally devastating effect (more on how hard a thrown knife hits later). A knife is a lot cheaper, surer (they don't jam or run out of ammo) safer, legal, and its quiet and, I add a bit whimsically, more *sporting* than a handgun. Now let me say that if anybody broke into my place to steal my few belongings; they can have the stuff before I toss a blade at them.

But if my family, or my vintage accordion are threatened, I believe it appropriate for me to make an aggressive defense. Maybe the old adage "don't bring a knife to a gun fight" is true most of the time, but, as a personal choice, I am not keeping a loaded and charged pistol about my place. A hefty knife, on the other hand, is always charged and loaded in the hands of an expert thrower. This all could be argued; either way I don't advocate violence of any sort. Knife throwing to me is a challenging and rewarding sport owning certain collateral martial applications that I hope I'll never have to apply.

Chapter One

Safety First and Always
It's All Fun – till Somebody Get's Hurt!

One lazy summer day a few years back, I was in my backyard doing some knife throwing and was curious as to just how hard a thrown knife actually hits its target. To find out, I chose a thick piece of plywood (not a recommended target material) and I took my knife, the Camillus (same one through the years) and gripping it firmly, I came at it in an overhand swing some call the "Comanche style" knife attack. At the time, I was a man of above average strength and when I stabbed that plywood as hard as I could, that knife buried in perhaps a half an inch – but it didn't go through. I did this several times with the same results. Next, I stood back maybe 10 or 15 feet and threw the same knife at it and the blade punched clean through. Several more throws resulted in similar results.

Because plywood is a relatively hard target (and subsequently **NOT** recommended as suitable target material), the blade was actually warm from the hits. I was impressed. I was also more appreciative that one could expect a thrown knife that hits flesh to bury to the hilt unless it hits a bone – and then expect it to seriously damage that bone – no joking.

This is a sport with very lethal potential. Respect this as I hope you would with a loaded gun. Knife throwing has undoubtedly gotten untold thousands of people accidentally killed over the ages – with not a few of these accidents involving alcohol. Any thrown knife has definite lethal, blood-letting potential.

1. Make Sure the Target Area is Clear of People, Pets, and Valuables

First and foremost let anybody in the area know you are throwing a knife and at what you are throwing it. Make sure all people, pets, and breakables are well clear of the area.

2. What Happened to Tom Can Happen to Anybody

When I met my high school friend Tom, he was blind in both eyes. One day, I got around to asking him how he became blind. To this he answered:

"I was born blind in one eye. A few years ago I was throwing a knife and it bounced back and put my other eye out."

Talk about bad luck! I asked him if he was serious and he assured me that he was. Bad luck happens. But you can reduce the odds of bad luck striking you by staying aware and practicing safe throwing standards.

I've lost count of how many times I've had to do a quick dance to avoid getting hit by knives that ricocheted off targets. Knives bouncing back or flying wild pose the second biggest hazard in knife throwing:
The biggest hazard is poor judgment.

> **Anticipate Bounce-back Trajectory**
>
> A bad throw at a flat surface (like a wall) will send the blade straight back at you. Whereas a bad throw at an irregular-shaped target (like a tree) could send the bounce-back knife in any direction. These things happen in this sport – and are something to anticipate and be aware of.

3. Don't Throw at Targets Too Hard to Stick a Knife In

Just like a bullet or a 120mm depleted-uranium tank round, your knife will have its limits on what it can and can not effectively penetrate. Be aware that throwing at targets made of hard material poise risks to the thrower, his environment, and last but not least - the knife. Hard target material includes: metals, plywood, dried and cured hardwoods, or a softer, smaller target with metal or concrete around it (where you might throw wild and hit the metal or concrete)

The thrown knife must obey the known laws of physics:

All that thrown kinetic energy is going somewhere – if the target isn't absorbing it, then the energy will remain with the knife and it will either shatter or bounce back.

4. Don't Throw Knives and Other Implements that are Too Hard and Brittle

Metal files come to mind – they throw and stick great but are too brittle and break and shatter easily. Also too hard and brittle are many older knives made of high carbon steel (often grey in color); these take and hold a very fine razor edge and are highly sought after by collectors.(see chapter two). If you really must throw these kinds of knives, I strongly recommend softer targets for routine practice (see chapter on targets).

5. An Impaired Mind can Become an Impaled Mind

OK, we all know this: The same rules that apply to firearms and intoxicants apply to knife throwing and intoxicants. Here's the *other* thing; if you don't drink – beware of knife throwers that do.

Nothing like a really stupid accident to completely ruin a good time.

Do yourself justice by not being the party goon that hurt somebody bad from throwing knives. A dulled mind is like a dull knife – worthless when it's needed – sometimes dangerous to self and others when in use.

Confession: On the night of my fortieth birthday, my hand-made Spanish guitar took a knife through the soundboard due to my own carelessness. This had a pronounced negative effect upon the guitar's sound and appearance and rendered the vintage instrument pretty much worthless.

6. Your Clothes Make a Big Difference

The act of throwing a knife engages the entire body into one focused motion. Restrictive clothing has a tremendous impact upon your throwing abilities. This isn't saying you can't throw well with restrictive clothing on; but you will have to mentally compensate for these factors if you are to hit *and* stick your intended target. Less restrictive clothing is significantly desirable for knife throwing. So ultimately, it goes to reason that if you are throwing at your best – then the chances of a dangerous wild throw are reduced. This isn't to say that the ideal throwing attire is nude or in a thong and sandals.

Clothing does offer *some* protection from bounce backs. A stray bounce-back that hits my boot is far better than it hitting my bare foot.

7. Beware of the "Other" Knife Throwers

Surprise! You and I aren't the only ones addicted to knife throwing! Chances are others will see you throwing and want to get in on the fun and show their stuff. They always do – and they rarely know what they are doing. You've seen these types in action: they throw wild and hope it sticks. Don't look down on them, at some point in time that is what we were until we evolved into skilled knife throwers. So, with this in mind; watch out for the bad judgment and wild throws of the others.

What two things do bayonets and screwdrivers have in common?

Because throwing many different knives and items is encouraged, some things deserve special mention because they come with inherent risks qualities.

1. As throwing implements, both bayonets and screwdrivers are virtually indestructible and pointy and throw well.

2. They are also both highly prone to bounce straight back at you with unusual force - more so, in my throwing experience, than any other throwing implement. I don't know why this is, can only guess it's in the temper of steel, but if you throw either of these items - be extra prepared to evade an aggressive bounce back - coming at ya! Ha!

Chapter Two

Knives and Other Sharp Things to Throw

There must be at least a thousand types of knife blades. For the purposes of this book, the most common blade types will be evaluated for their ability to be thrown and withstand repeated throwing. However, before any discussion on knife type and evaluation can be made, we need to get on the same sheet of music on knife design, construction and terminology.

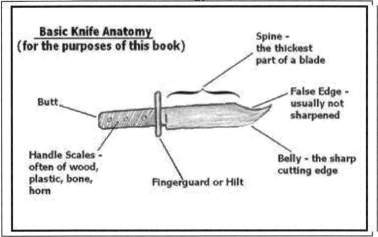

The ever-changing English language

The word *knife*, with it's now silent "k", as all words with the silent "k", is an old word in the English lexicon that goes back to the days of the knights of Arthur's legendary table. The invading, and ultimately successful, Viking Norsemen called such a cutting and stabbing tool and weapon a "knifr". The English language subsequently adopted the word and spelled it "cnif". Back then, the "k" and "c" letters would have been pronounced, as in "k-neef". Add the "e" to make the present form of the word "knife", and it was pronounced "k-neefa". Point is that words associated with such an ancient yet common word as "knife" are many. Is it a quillon, a hilt, a hand guard, or a finger guard? Knowing the etymology of the word "knife" won't make you a better thrower – just a more knowledgeable thrower.

The Cutting Edge and Blade Strength

A throwing knife is functionally a spear with a very short handle.

You certainly can throw any knife and stick a target. However, if you are looking to buy knives solely for repeated knife throwing at hard and soft targets, then to a small degree the blade's cutting edge grind comes into some consideration as the edge grind can effect the strength of the blade when used as a throwing implement.

What follows are the four primary ways knife makers grind and hone blade edges – each depending upon the intended use of the knife.

Four Basic Ways Knife Edges are Ground

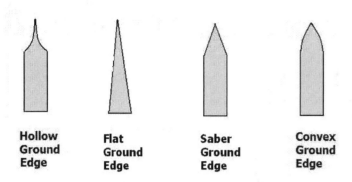

Hollow-Ground Edge: This is the sharpest – but structurally weakest of the four – and can literally be made razor sharp. However, it is the easiest to dull and break. Straight razors and many chef knives are hollow ground. If a person knows how to properly sharpen a hollow-ground edge, they'll easily take their excellent razor edge back. However, in the hands of a novice sharpener, the edge can be further dulled or even badly damaged. These knives are specifically made for shaving, slicing and dicing and not stabbin and jabbin (and throwing).

I've never been cut throwing a knife, but then I have never thrown a knife with a razor-sharp edge. If you throw a sharp-edged blade, hold it with the sharp edge facing *out* – as in the illustration on different grips. This common-sense advice is akin to not pissing in the wind: but most of us have done that at some time - haven't we?

Flat-Ground Edge: Another very-sharp blade grind and generally a bit stronger than the hollow-ground blade. Though not quite as sharp as a hollow-ground edge, these knives will take a fine edge and hold an edge just a little better than most hollow-ground knives – and are easier to sharpen. Still, such blades are on the weak side for extended and hard use as throwing knives.

Saber-Ground Edge: This will moderately take and hold an edge. In terms of sharpness and strength, the saber-ground falls between the flat ground and convex. Many edged carpentry tools are saber ground. These are well suited for hard and regular throwing purposes in that the edge will hold up to the hard abuse that throwing places on a knife.

Convex-Ground Edge – the strongest – and generally dullest of edges: hatchets and axes have convexly-ground edges. A very suitable tool for hacking and whacking – chopping and lopping, but not so good at slicing and dicing. A knife with such a convex-ground blade would be ideal for repeated throwing use.

Blade grind is not a huge factor in choosing throwing knives as you can throw any knife regardless of the blade grind – just know that the sharper, more delicate blades might have their edge damaged or the blade broken after repeated throwing and you need to take care not to slice your hand in the blade-held throws. It's no big deal – just something to be aware of.

Knife Metals
Knife metal has vastly improved in relatively recent years. Consider that all our ancestors were using knives of bone and flinty rock for untold ages before copper came into the scene as a valuable knife material. Around the world, at

different places and times, curious blacksmiths eventually discovered that adding tin to copper made a new and stronger metal and thus the alloy bronze came in, which was better than copper for blades, but not that much better. The Bronze Age lasted roughly two thousand years while more blacksmith geniuses were tampering with and refining techniques for smelting and making iron. The process for smelting iron infuses a small percent (3 or 4%) of carbon – which makes the iron harder but brittle (not good for knife throwing).

The refinement of iron into steel was perhaps the greatest technological advance for knife throwing since the very first ape man got the right combination of brain cells to put it all together to throw and stick pointy things. So at different times and places, people learned to purify the iron by removing some of the carbon through various refined smelting techniques and steel was born – a hard but not brittle metal well suited for weapons and tools and for knife throwing.

The man wielding a *steel* sword had a deciding edged advantage over the man wielding his grandfather's prized copper or bronze tally whacker. In this way, many a copper sword collected from earth's old battlefields were melted down and remade into plow shares, a stylish helmet, or better yet: a shiny new copper frying pan for the victorious warrior's woman.

In the past hundred years, advances in metallurgy have sped up greatly. Modern tanks have armor of ceramic alloys. There are in recent years super hard and razor sharp knives also made of ceramic alloys (too brittle for throwing). But by far most knives are made of some variant of steel.

Steel: High Carbon or Non-High-Carbon

> **NON-STAINLESS, HIGH-CARBON STEELS**
>
> Technically speaking, steels with between 1.0 – 2.0% carbon content are classified as high-carbon steel and are able to be tempered to very hard levels.

Non-stainless, high-carbon steel kitchen cutlery
You will know these blades as they will discolor gray and/or rust. Like cast-iron pans, these sharp blades need to be heated and dried after each use and washing. Why go through all the trouble? Why not get a blade of stainless steel? These often large and heavy blades can be hand-honed to wicked razor-sharp edges. Often far more expensive than stainless cutlery, they make great butcher knives and cleavers.

Advise not to throw these as they will not hold up to the impact shock against hard targets (such as wood) before breaking and becoming at best garbage - at worst an injury. Of course, if you are throwing at much softer targets, such brittle throwing implements should do fine without breaking.

Non-stainless, high-carbon steel tools – ALL files, both wood and metal files, are too hard and will shatter. As with knives of high-carbon construction, the grey metal color usually indicates high-carbon metal.

> **STAINLESS STEELS**
> **(AKA "INOX" for French Inoxydable"):**
>
> These steels will not easily oxidize (rust) and are corrosion resistant due to the addition of at least 10.5% chromium to the steel. Stainless steel knives came into western markets via European developers around 1915. Stainless steel may or may not be high carbon steel.

Stainless Steel blades that are not high carbon– knives of stainless steel that are not of high-carbon material are generally fine for repeated throwing as they are not too brittle. Fortunately for the knife thrower, it seems that the majority of knives (both cheap and expensive) are made of vastly varying grades of non-high-carbon stainless steel.

Ceramic-alloy blades – these have blades with sharp edges that are very hard to dull. (and sharpen). Their weakness is that they are so hard as to snap or shatter when used in a prying motion or thrown. These blades usually are relatively expensive.

The Short and Long of the Topic:
Throwing Knife Metals
Volumes could be written about metal and how it relates to a good throwing knife. In my 35 years of throwing, I have learned that most of the less expensive knives are made of

relatively softer grades of stainless steel and make durable throwing knives. Thing is, even if they do break, the loss of a cheap, mass produced knife isn't going to break your heart or wallet. Shop for some inexpensive knives you like with <u>full tang construction</u> and modify them into a great thrower that will last.

Folding Knives: Lock blades, Switchblades, Butterfly knives
Lockblades, switchblades, bolo knives – <u>DO NOT</u> throw these at hard targets (trees, plywood, etc) or the next throw will be into the garbage can. They will break to pieces: the blade, handle, pins and springs – all of it – garbage. These knives are held together by pins and screws and will not survive a thrown impact upon a hard target. OK, you've been warned. This brings us to the next critically important topic on the subject of throwing knife construction and design – the knife's handle *tang*.

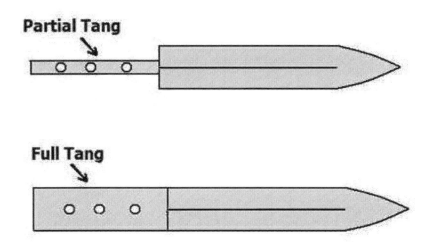

Full Tang Construction Prevents Throwing Knife Destruction

The "tang" in a knife is the metal half that extends from the blade section into the handle section.

In terms of throwing knife design and construction, the matter of a knife being full-tang or partial tang construction is very critical IF you plan to keep throwing the same knife into target as hard as wood.

A full-tang blade will hold up to the repeated hard impact of being thrown for years whereas a partial-tang constructed knife WILL eventually break at the hilt - sometimes only after a few throws.

HOWEVER, this is certainly not to say you can't throw and hit *and* stick a partial-tang knife as well as a full-tang. ALSO, if you are throwing at targets softer than wood (layered cardboard or soft organic material such as pumpkins etc.), the partial-tang throwing knife will do just fine, but thrown at harder-surfaced targets, typically of wood, expect the partial-tang knife to eventually break at the hilt rendering it worthless.

Spine: A Spineless Blade is a Weak Blade.
Most knife blades aren't uniform in thickness (unlike a putty knife or razor blade). The thicker part of a knife blade is aptly called the "spine" of the blade.

Like the full-tang or partial-tang construction of a knife you plan to use as a thrower, how strongly the spine reinforces the knife blade is something to consider. However, of the two, I would say a full-tang handle is more critical than the spine in a throwing knife's structural strength

Spine Placement and Blade Design: Will you be *Slicing and Dicing* or *Stabbing and Jabbing*?
A blade's spine is functionally situated to support the knife for its primary function – be it either cutting or penetrating. Sometimes, as in the clip-point blade, the knife is designed for both functions. The following illustrations show the different uses of a spine in blades.

Knife Areas Prone to Breakage When Thrown
Needle-point Stiletto Dagger

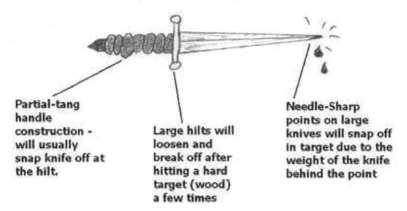

Partial-tang handle construction - will usually snap knife off at the hilt.

Large hilts will loosen and break off after hitting a hard target (wood) a few times

Needle-Sharp points on large knives will snap off in target due to the weight of the knife behind the point

In the needle-point stiletto dagger, though there is a strong spine running down the entire center length of the blade, the needle point and partial tang are both susceptible to breakage when thrown at hard targets of wood. Such knives as these throw well (in that you can control the spin well) and stick deep – but are only suitable for softer targets than wood.

Common Flatback Blade

Flatback blades, such as the one depicted above, have hollow or flat-ground blades. They generally are very sharp with the business end being the blade's edge (rather than the point). Therefore the spine is along the top part of the blade to support downward pressure on the blade and also

safely allow you to press down on the blade with your hand if need be (as if you were going to pare or dice food on a cutting block). These can make good throwing knives. But unless the blade is reasonably thick, it could break.

Curved-edge Blade

Cutlass-like curved-edge knives have long, sharp bellies that are made for slashing and skinning and as such would typically have a flat-ground blade. With a pointy tip, the curved-edge blade is highly susceptible to break if thrown. Such a knife, as the one depicted above with a finger-grooved handle and a large pommel (butt), would have a partial-tang construction and would break at the hilt. Throw this only if your life depends upon it – or you just hate this knife.

Clip-point Blade on a Large Bowie

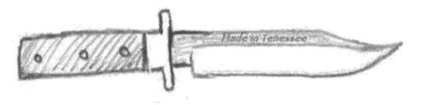

The Bowie-style blade is made for a dual purpose of slicing and dicing and stabbing and jabbing. As such, the spine is usually very strong (thick) and runs the length of the blade to the point (depicted in the shaded areas on the blade of the Bowie above).

With a strong spine and full-tang handle – these make great and sturdy throwing knives. Just the same, the fancy hilt and the wood or bone handle scales will break off eventually (not effecting the throwing capabilities of this knife) and should be removed or modified.

Spear-point Blade

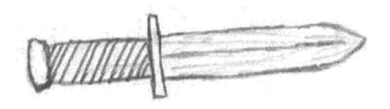

As the name suggests, the spear point blade is intended for spearing targets and, like the dagger, has a strong spine running the course of the blade. Many knives classified as "boot knives" have thickly-spined spear-point blades. Usually boot knives are smaller and are good for closer range (indoor) throwing. If you can find some of these boot knives that are full-tang construction, and cheap, buy a few as they would make decent, durable throwing knives. Many "professional" throwing knives (knives sold explicitly as throwing knives) are spear-point design.

Spearpoint Blade on a "Professional" Throwing Knife

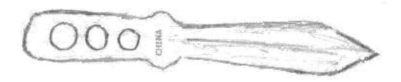

Other Sharp Things That Throw Great
Hatchets, Tomahawks, Axes

Though this is beyond the scope of this book, I will say that hatchets, tomahawks, and axes throw great and have great range and utterly devastating striking power. Because of the handle and weight proportions, it is relatively easy to control the spin of these war-like weapons. They will massacre just about any target. One could big game hunt with tomahawks and hatchets (don't know if that's legal or not). When thrown often at hard targets (such as trees), they tend to break where the wooden handle meets the metal head. Also, bear in mind that with all their weight and boomerang-like form, hatchets, axes and tomahawks REALLY fly wild and far when they don't hit and stick - so be careful!

Back in the "olden days", I imagine a lot of Vikings and American Indian warriors were maimed from wild or boomerang tomahawk hatchet and ax throws made by their friends. The un-cool warrior is the outcast who accidently killed or maimed his comrade.

Meat Cleavers

Sometimes, I get a "wild hair" and want to throw something *different*. In such times I'll reach for an old favorite throwing item; a heavy, full-tang construction meat cleaver. I have several large cleavers hanging in my kitchen; and I am pretty handy with them. Half knife – half hatchet; they throw great - have great range (both near and far), hit extremely hard, and are, in my opinion, the easiest throwing item (named in this book) to throw and control the spin. Grasp one by the handle and throw it with the same principles laid down in chapter five for knife throwing. The handle and weight of the blade give you a certain favorable leverage in spin control. Cleavers will pulverize a target just like an axe or hatchet.
Cleavers are also pretty damn handy at making quick work at lopping off fish and chicken heads or chopping up venison.

IMPORTANT: Make sure the cleavers you buy have full-tang handle construction. You can tell by looking at the handle – if the handle is round it's certainly partial-tang. If it's flat sided, it *probably* has a full-tang handle. Those like the one depicted in this book, with large rivets or screws holding wood handle scales on, would have a full-tang construction.

Nails – Big Hand-Sharpened Ones

Once, I bought some really big nails - like foot-long nails. My original intent was to use them as tent stakes but figured they might throw pretty well as well; my hunch was right. I ground and filed the sharp end into tapered needle-sharp points (like a knitting needle) and these babies were very good (and cheap) throwing items - for closer ranges. I had about a dozen of them that I was whipping into just about everything wood and stationary for a while. They hit and plant into a target with a strangely gratifying "Tok!" sound; whip another three in quick succession "Tok! – Tok! – Tok!"- music!. Outdoors, they easily get lost. I don't know what happened to mine. Hope nobody stepped on them. In hindsight, I recommend painting such items a florescent color.

A Few Words on Knife Balance

The "Perfectly-Balanced Professional" Throwing Knife?

"Professional" throwing knives are knives that are specifically designed and sold as throwing knives and are usually advertised as perfectly balanced for throwing. Such knives are often virtually indestructible in their one-piece, full-tang stainless steel construction – with no hilt or handle materials.

I have long pondered and questioned the actual merits of the advertised "well" or even "perfectly" balanced throwing knife. The question that it always comes down to is; *perfectly balanced to whose arm and throwing style?*

I have seen novice throwers claim that if you can balance a knife on your finger at the hilt, it is "perfectly" balanced and perfect for throwing. This is childish nonsense; a knife that has a blade heavier than the handle (as most knives are) is easier to control than these "balanced" throwing knives: this is my opinion and experience (and my knife-throwing brother's opinion as well). I advocate obtaining knives of different kinds and sizes: boot knives, bowie knives, combat knives, hunting knives and cleavers – so long as they have a full-tang handle – strip them down to make a fine collection of custom throwers for all occasions (see chapter 3).

You Have a Very Precise Weight Scale Issued at Birth
The gold does not determine the weight of the scale it rests upon. Likewise, it's not the knife that makes the perfect balance; but the hand that wields it.

FACT: We are all born with a weight scale and calculator somewhere in our brains. You will, as a knife thrower, gradually develop your mental weight scale and balance to a much finer degree than the general population. Be aware of it.

As a thrower, when you pick a knife up for the first time, you are "balancing" it with your eyes by visually sizing up its mass and proportions while your hand and arm heft it a few times so you get a feel for its center of balance - all this comes naturally. Your hand, arm, eyes and mind work together like a highly capable weight scale and you will know and memorize any given knife's balance properties in relation to throwing it. All in practice! Knowing this makes me look at the "perfectly balanced" professional throwing knives with comical disdain.

Recently, I spoke with my brother (who has been throwing as long as I) who is teaching his son the finer points of precision knife throwing. They went out and bought a bunch of balanced "throwing" knives. He was telling me these things did anything but throw well. To this, I personally agreed. Based on my own experience, a knife that is blade heavy will throw better as you have the weight/balance leverage to better control the spin in flight.

On the other hand, it must be said that "professional" balanced throwing knives are made to last in that they are soft-grade stainless steel and full-tang construction with no hilts or pommel to hang up. Such knives do have their merits.

A competent knife thrower (a man for any occasion) can pick up any given knife, throw it, and stick it. A few hefts in the hand and a visual and mental appraisal are all that is needed to "balance" any throwing knife. It's all part of the sport!

Size Matters in Throwing Knives
The fundamentals of how to throw any given knife remain the same regardless of the size. However, the trajectory, spin, and hitting characteristics between large knives and smaller knives are considerable.

Larger Throwing Knives: knives with blades over 6"
- Longer throwing range;
- Larger knives generally spin less than smaller, lighter knives and are easier to control the spin;
- Larger knives hit a target very hard and have greater "take down" power;
- They are well suited for throwing by the handle and for farther ranges;
- Larger knives take more room to throw - and aren't well suited for most indoor "situations";
- Larger knives will tear up most targets fast.

Smaller Throwing Knives
- Tend to spin more than larger knives (but you can compensate for this with practice);
- Often best suited for throwing by the blade at close to medium ranges;
- Smaller throwing knives will not chew up a target as fast as a larger blade; are easier to conceal; more suitable for most indoor throwing situations;
- A smaller blade still hits hard and penetrates deep - sufficient for most target situations - though not with as much devastation as a larger blade.

For these reasons, perfect your throwing game with blades of all sizes. If you are throwing outdoors, you have your large knives. If throwing indoors, you have your small knives. You are a man (or woman) for all occasions.

Chapter Three

Collecting and Modifying Throwing Knives

One enjoyable aspect of knife throwing is simply collecting knives. You know there are thousands of knives to obtain; most quite affordable. So my advise to you; start collecting knives of varying size and style that are cheap and have full-tang construction; if it has a strongly-spined blade – all the better.

So long as the knife is full-tang construction, chances are, you can make a very decent thrower out of it. This is also where you can customize a lot of formerly el-cheapo blades into items that are a personal extension of your knife-thrower image. Your customizations will also be utilitarian and functional.

Two Things a Throwing Knife Will Shed: With or Without Your Help
The Hilt
Hilts serve a purpose when using a knife to cut or stab to protect your grip from slipping forward from the handle onto the blade - ouch! Bloody mess! Hilts protect your knife-holding hand in other ways as well. In a knife fight against another knife-wielding whacko, the hilt also serves the function of paring your opponent's knife slashes that

invariably contact your blade. Such slashes, if there is no hilt, would travel down your blade to your hand and cause a nasty deep hand wound and maybe make you drop your knife and leave you wide open for a more lethal (and maybe final) follow-up attack. With the hilt in place, your hand would be blocked from the bad guy or woman's slashing blade and the fight continues; unless, of course, you make a peace offering of a smile and jelly beans. Jellybeans throw well too and if you chew them a little – they stick great!

In palm-held throws, a large hilt will catch some on your hand and cause you to lose control of the spin. For this reason, large hilts should be ground or cut down to a minimal size. Sand all cut or filed surfaces smooth with emery cloth or a fine file. If you don't remove the hilt, it will break off anyway after a number of throws at any target of wood. Also for consideration: because it will be flying and spinning, you also want the throwing knife to be as sleek and aerodynamic in form as possible. If you only plan to throw the knife, remove the hilt. If the knife has duel purposes, just reduce the hilt.

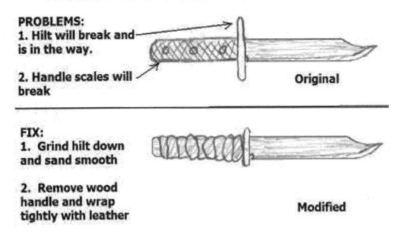

The Handle

Knife handle materials on full-tang knives are there to improve grip and for appearance. To this end, they serve a good purpose. However, most knives will shed the handle material before too long when thrown repeatedly into target of wood. The only handle material that comes to mind that won't be shed after many throws is the stacked leather disks that make up the venerable old USMC KaBar and the old USAF Pilots Survival Knife (by the now sadly closed Camillus knife factory). Many, if not most, knife handles are held on by rivets, pins, or screws. The impact of a knife thrown into a harder target is so great that these rivets, pins, or screws will break, or the handle, will break off leaving exposed rivets, pins, or screws which will catch on your throwing hand causing a missed throw - and such broken handles look ugly.

Of course, if you are throwing at targets softer than wood, your knife handles will be spared and can stay in place. Otherwise, handles need to be removed or wait and they will remove themselves after a routine throwing use.
To remove most handles, first remove the handle material by sawing or filing them off. Next, file or cut the handle pins down flush with the tang or drill or punch them out.

Once the handle material and pins are removed, you can leave the tang bare or wrap it with leather or any other material you choose. Wrapping the handle does not enhance the knife as a throwing implement, but if you need to use the knife for anything besides throwing, a handle is desirable for grip. Custom-wrapped handles also look good and it transforms your throwing knife from another cheap mass-produced item into your own work of art - your personalized tool, toy and weapon. You know what I mean. Again, go shopping for some really cheap knives of different sizes that have full-tang construction and modify them into custom throwing knives. In catalogs and online, the knife description will not often say if it is full-tang construction or not, but you can usually figure it out by looking at it.

Chapter Four

Targets

What's to say about targets? Cheese and crackers! Anything within your throwing range is a potential target! Just the same, the one main concern on target selection (aside from it being lawful and morally responsible to throw a knife at) is Safety: safety to you, safety to your knife, safety to those around you, and lastly - safety to your target. Using my own past as the 'bad' example: you don't want to do like I did in younger years and tear up things like doors and walls winging knives into them as this makes for expensive damage, is often unsafe, and tends to get the wife, girlfriend, and property owner decidedly non-supportive of your knife throwing *thing*. Target decisions abound. Whatever you do: be safe.

Two Main Types of Targets:
Hard and anchored targets: trees and building walls are examples. These targets are hard (as in dense) and will not move or give when hit by a knife.

Softer and/or not anchored targets: Layered cardboard, pumpkins, targets of wood suspended on chains or rope, wild game, bad guys, bad guy car or motor-scooter tires and etc. These are softer than trees or walls and will move (give) some when hit with a knife.

In short, hard targets last longer and there are trees and wooden walls everywhere; but they are hard on knives. I was joking about the "bad guy" stuff but you get the idea.

A Recommended Indoor Target

Build a large layered cardboard target with pine board backing as it is ideal for indoor throwing with smaller knives as well as knives you wish to practice with that are not of full-tang or durable construction. Cardboard targets also retard bounce-backs so you don't have bad throws zinging off targets indoors. Replace cardboard as needed. These make great targets.

Indoor Target of Layered Cardboad Attached to a Pine Backing

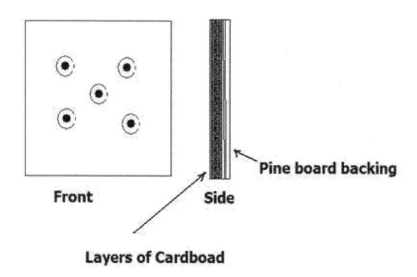

A Recommended Outdoor Target

With not much more effort, and you if live in the country and wield a chainsaw or know somebody that does, you can make an excellent and durable semi-soft target by cutting and suspending a cross section of a tree log on a couple chains or rope attached to a couple eye bolts. This target will serve you well and last a long, *long* time. If it wears out, toss it in the party fire pit, suspend another cross section, and have at it. Yes, the illustration is cheesy, but the target is good.

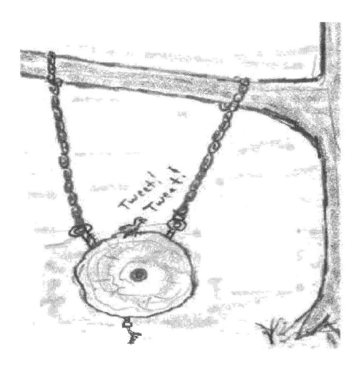

Trees

In this hyper-sensitive day and age, some will question: Is it morally irresponsible to damage trees for sport? Is it? I doubt that few who would read this book would be asking this. But you know there are those who would be upset at using a living tree as a knife target. Keeping an open mind, I say 'maybe they are *right*'. Not that that ever stopped me from using trees as knife targets; unless it was one of my dad's trees. I always felt that if a tree had thoughts, maybe it would be honored to have me select it as a worthy target. Could be worse, I could have targeted it with a chain saw. I guess this is just another reason to love trees.

However…
If you throw and miss the tree altogether, or it bounces off the side in a bad throw, where's your knife going? At this point, you will have lost positive control over your knife and must accept the consequences; come as they may. While wild throws at a wall will predictably send the knife STRAIGHT back at the thrower, wild throws at a tree can send a knife flying anywhere.

Chapter Five

Throwing Techniques

Factors in Making the Knife Hit - *Point First*
1. **Lady Luck**: Fickle and flippant luck can help you hit the target. But Lady Luck is an unreliable wench and is our friend one moment and suddenly gone off to the next guy without warning.

2. **Spin Control**: This is what it's all about: you controlling the spin of your knife - any knife - so that it hits the target point first. Factors in spin control are:

a) Shoulder, elbow, and wrist movements of your throwing arm.
b) Posture
c) Range assessment
d) Knife assessment (in terms of the knife's weight and balance)

Other books on knife throwing incorporate loads of photos of a person (presumably the author) throwing a knife to indicate proper throwing posture and arm movement. To this I argue that nobody needs to be shown or told how to throw something. Throwing is about as natural as walking. If throwing is awkward for you to do (for whatever reason); limber up with some stretches and gradually work your way into throwing with greater range and ease. Throw a knife in whatever way is natural and comfortable for your own arm: making it hit point first is the challenge to focus upon.

In terms of spin control, you will need to train your throwing arm to work with your mental range and knife balance assessment to make the knife hit point first.

The Wrist
Of everything going on with your throwing arm, how much you move or don't move the wrist will affect the spin of your knife the most.

As a rule for both handle and blade-held throws, *more wrist movement equals more spin*. At close ranges requiring the blade to spin, this is desirable. At farther ranges, a more rigid, unmoving throwing wrist will be wanted. With practice, you will eventually make these adjustments automatically without thinking about them - *with practice*.

In so far as the throwing movements of the elbow, shoulder, and body go - do what is natural and comfortable to you in throwing. Focus on the wrist - and the grip and release.

The Grip and the Release
How many spins are needed between you and the target? The answer to this will also depend much upon how you grip and release the knife.

1. Blade grip
2. Handle Grip
3. Palmed

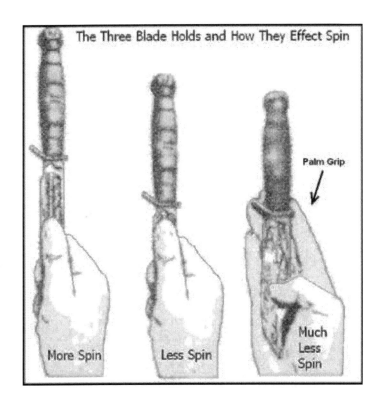

Blade Grip Throws

The blade grip is a basic grip for "flip" throws - and this will suffice for the majority of throwing situations. A handy thing about holding the knife on the blade when throwing it is that you can greatly affect the rate of spin by choking up or down on the blade.

If you choke up - that is; if you hold the blade up closer to the handle - it will not spin as quite much. Choking down the blade towards the tip will make the blade spin more.

Handle Grip Throws

When throwing a knife by a handle grip, the knife must make at least one complete 360 degree turn between you and the target. This requires a little more practice than the blade grip flip throw - but this also can increase your effective range over the blade-held flip throw. Throwing by the handle is also more suitable for larger knives.

Mastering throwing a knife by the handle takes more practice than getting the blade-held throw down - but once you have it down, you might find it to be the preferred method for the majority of your throws. It's all a matter of preference.

Palm Grip Throws

With the palm grip, you are holding the knife by the blade but in such a manner that you have essentially choked up on the knife as far as possible. Advantage: Range. Disadvantage: for some, the precision and accuracy of the throw. With all techniques, try it and see what works best for you. Some throwing techniques work better with different knives and situations.

The Release

It comes as no surprise that the way you are gripping your knife at the moment it is released will significantly influence the spin of the knife. I guess another way to word this is; the way your release a knife will effect the spin.

If you let the knife *glide* smoothly straight out of your hand upon release, you will get less spin. Think of a knife blade being withdrawn straight out of a loose-fitting scabbard.

If you desire more spin for closer ranges, grip the knife just a bit firmer with the fingers to exercise control on the spin. Mentally envision the amount of spin you require.

Objects that can adversely alter your release control occur when the knife and hand get held up on rings or large knife hilts on palm-grip throws.

The Speed and Force of the Throw
A harder, faster thrown knife will spin less in its flight to a target. If you need to throw the knife hard at something but it is close range, compensate for this and deliberately put a bit more spin to it with a "snap" of the wrist. On the other hand, if all you have mastered is the half-turn flip throw, and a given target is a bit out of your normal range, try throwing harder and see if that compensates by reducing the spin.

Be aware also that while you are learning, you're going to miss some and a faster thrown knife bounces back all that much faster! Comin at ya!

If You Can Mentally "See" It First: You Can Do It.
This goes with so many things in life. This may be **The Big Trick** to successful knife throwing. If you can mentally envision what exactly it is you are trying to get the knife to do, before you throw, it will be that much easier to accomplish. With this in mind, try these training aids – see if they help:

Walk The Blade To The Target: doing this can greatly help your mind to fully envision and grasp what it must do - walk your knife through what you want it to do. That is, from your throwing position, slowly walk the knife to the target, turning the knife slowly with your hands as you walk just the way it must spin (a half turn, or full turn etc.) until the point reaches the target. You know how the blade must be at the halfway point between you and your target (see illustrations on half-turn and full-turn throws), so use the halfway point as your reference as you walk and turn the knife – manually replicating how it must spin in its journey to the target.

Do this until you get a feel for what you are trying to make the knife do; take special note of how it must turn between your throwing position and the halfway point - then go throw. With practice, you will not need to walk the blade to the target as your mind will be able to make these assessments and adjustments comfortably and automatically.

Mentally Cut the Range in Half: Envision how you want the blade to be HALFWAY between you and your target. This might simplify the mental task of envisioning what it is you want to make the knife do. If the knife is pointing as it should halfway between you and the target, the knife will continue on to hit point first (see illustrations on half-turn and full-turn throws).

The Basic Half-turn "Flip" Throw - for Blade and Palm Held Throws Only

RANGE: SHORT TO MEDIUM
This is the easiest and most rudimentary throw to learn and is a basic throwing technique used only for throws made by gripping or palming the knife by the blade. Basic as it is, it will still fully suffice for most throwing situations out to 25 feet or so - depending upon your skill and your knife.
With the half-turn flip throw, you are simply flipping the blade over once into the target.

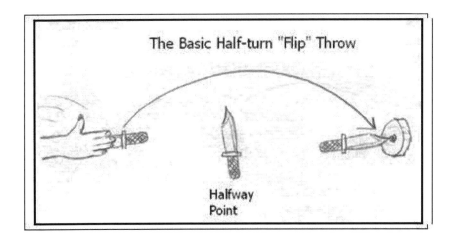

Use the half-turn flip throw when holding the knife by the blade or palming the blade. This throw will suffice for most throwing situations.

Once Again: Try to visualize how you want the knife at the halfway range (blade pointing up) – this may help – walk it to the target a few times until you mentally get comfortable with what you are going to make the knife accomplish.

The 360 Full-Turn Throw - For Handle-held Throws
RANGE: MEDIUM TO LONG
The advantage of throwing a knife by the handle is that it can fairly double your range over the half turn flip throw.

Full-Turn Throw

The full-turn throw is a handle-held throw - longer range than the half-turn throw.

*Tip! Once you have mastered the basic half-turn "flip" throw, mentally estimate the half-way point between your target and you and flip the knife a half turn so that the handle is pointing at you at the half-way point: the knife will hit the target point first.

Other Throws

While the half turn and full turn throws are enough to meet almost all throwing situations, how about really far way targets? How about close quarter "combat" quick reaction throws? How about just adding more challenge to a great hobby?

The Double Full-Turn Throw - For *Far Out* Throwing Challenges

Once you have mastered the full turn throw, and if you feel a need to open the range up even further, then you can work on the double full-turn throw, which is of course TWO full turns of the knife between you and the target. Like the previously described throws, it may help to mentally cut the range in half – where at the half-way point the knife blade will be facing the target (if thrown by the handle). In my experience and opinion, this throw takes a high-degree of mental clarity, as well as acquired skill and practice.

The Combat Spear Throw

I call this throw a "combat" throw because I can't think of many sporting applications for it other than combat or reckless showing off. Suitable for close-ranges and smaller or medium-sized knives – sheathed boot and belt knives come to mind. It is a fast reaction close-range throw; out to 10 or 12 feet. I call it a "spear" throw because like a thrown spear, there is no spin in flight and you are throwing it point first. When mastered, this throw is something of a "quick draw" reaction throw – with force. Like a quick-draw gunshot, accuracy is somewhat sacrificed for speed.

CAUTION: Practice the Combat Spear Throw on softer targets as the force and close range of this throw put the thrower (and bystanders) in dangerous proximity to fast-moving bounce backs!

For this throw, <u>palm hold the knife</u> <u>by the handle</u> - with blade pointing out the same direction as your fingers. This would be just the way you would retrieve it from the sheath – by the handle.

In something like a quick slapping motion, briskly whip the knife at the target point first trying not to put any spin on the knife at all. Like the other throws, with practice you can extend your effective range.

Se how fast you can retrieve it from the sheath – be it boot or belt and safely and reliably stick a target.

Range Training Strategy

A simple strategy of advancing your effective knife-throwing range would follow:

1. Start with blade-held throws and master your half-turn throws with various knives and at various distances.

2. After mastering the half-turn blade throws, move on to handle-held throws and master the full-turn throws. These aren't so difficult if you start out by just trying to envision how you want the knife at the half-way point where the blade is now pointing towards you (see illustration). Envision what the knife must do in its flight to its target - walk it out to the target if you must, turning it as you go, to let your mind get a comfortable comprehension of what, exactly, it must do.

If you want to master whipping a boot or belt knife with speed at close ranges, practice the Combat Close-Range Spear Throw but on soft targets such as cardboard and get ready to move fast for bounce backs. Focus on getting the point to hit first – then work on accuracy. Keep Safety Top Priority!

Throwing in Darkness Alters Range Calculations

In an environment or situation where lighting is dim, be aware that your range calculations will be significantly challenged – if not off altogether. It's also harder to see a bounce back coming your way. What do you do about this? Avoid throwing in dark environments if you can.

If you must master throwing in darker environments for whatever reason, then practice by throwing in gradually increasing darker environments – but use very soft and giving targets where bounce backs will not occur. Perhaps a suspended, free-hanging layered cardboard (with pine backing) target would be ideal for maximum reduction in bounce backs. Safety glasses might not be a bad idea in such a risky training environment. It's also harder to find your poorly thrown knife in darker environments. Good luck!

Concluding Advice
Many people would have a beginner pace out to the target and practice throwing at set paces. This approach has the thrower learn to flip a knife into a target, at say seven paces, and add a pace of distance after mastering throwing at the previous pace count. This will work, though in my opinion, it is a really boring approach.

If you want to be a master thrower, you should learn to throw instinctively with all sorts of knives at any reasonable range. By "instinctively" I mean no set amount of paces or throwing with one type of knife. This will train your mind and body to pick up a given throwing implement, and while your arm and mind are calculating the weight and center of mass on what you are to throw, your eye and mind are calculating distance to target, clothing restrictions, and other factors: and you execute a precision throw – all with practice. Let safety become an instinctive calculation as well.

I can't say enough about mentally visualizing how your knife must spin. If it helps, physically walk the knife through its flight – turning it in your hand as you walk it to help train your mind as to exactly what it is you are requiring it to do with the throw.

Practice safe, practice often. Like any precision sport, you will have good days and bad days. No matter how good you get, the human condition we all share means that we can all do better – or worse. This makes life interesting, challenging and competitive.

May your steel never rust!

Printed in Great Britain
by Amazon